# BETHANY MOTA

## By Marie Morreale

Children's Press®
An Imprint of Scholastic Inc.

Photographs ©: cover: Christopher Polk/Getty Images for MTV; back cover: George Pimentel/Getty Images for Aeropostale; 1: Imeh Akpanudosen/Getty Images; 2: Frazer Harrison/Getty Images for Go Red; 3: Frazer Harrison/Getty Images for Go Red; 4-5: Bob Chamberlin/Los Angeles Times via Getty Images; 6-7: Rommel Demano/Getty Images; 8: Jerod Harris/Getty Images; 9: Dimitrios Kambouris/Getty Images for YouTube; 10: Laura Cavanaugh/Getty Images; 11: Taylor Hill/Getty Images; 12: Taylor Hill/Getty Images; 13: Timothy Hiatt/Getty Images for Aeropostale; 14: Everett Collection/Newscom; 15 top left: Shmonika/Shutterstock, Inc.; 15 top right: Jaguar PS/Shutterstock, Inc.; 15 center: Globe Turner/Shutterstock, Inc.; 15 bottom: Globe Turner/Shutterstock, Inc.; 16: Kristina Bumphrey, Starpix/AP Images; 17 top left: Dave Kotinsky/Getty Images; 17 top right: Donato Sardella/Getty Images for Louis Vuitton; 17 center: Photos 12/Alamy Images; 17 bottom left: Matt Cuda/Dreamstime; 17 bottom center: Scisetti Alfio/Fotolia; 17 bottom right: Everett Collection/Alamy Images; 18: Frazer Harrison/Getty Images; 21 top: Angela Weiss/Getty Images for Variety; 21 bottom: Timothy Hiatt/Getty Images for Aeropostale; 22: Sara Jaye Weiss/Startraks Photo; 23 top: George Pimentel/Getty Images for Aeropostale; 23 bottom: Charley Gallay/Getty Images for DCP; 24 top: Adam Taylor/ABC via Getty Images; 24 bottom: Rick Davis/Corbis Images; 25: Timothy Hiatt/Getty Images for Aeropostale; 27: Peter Kramer/NBC/NBC NewsWire via Getty Images; 28: Taylor Hill/Getty Images; 30: Astrid Stawiarz/Getty Images for Go Red; 31: Imeh Akpanudosen/Getty Images for ELLE; 32: Rommel Demano/Getty Images; 33: Noel Vasquez/Getty Images; 35: Timothy Hiatt/Getty Images for Aeropostale; 36 top left: Hong Vo/Shutterstock, Inc.; 36 top right: Viktor/Fotolia; 36 bottom: valery121283/Fotolia; 36-41 background: conejota/Thinkstock; 36 blue paper background and throughout: Nonnakrit/Shutterstock, Inc.; 36 pushpins and throughout: seregam/Thinkstock; 37 top: C Flanigan/Getty Images; 37 center: Tarek El Sombati/iStockphoto; 37 bottom: ronstik/Fotolia; 37 lined paper and throughout: My Life Graphic/Shutterstock, Inc.; 38 top: bentrussell/iStockphoto; 38 center: EdStock/iStockphoto; 38 bottom: Timothy Hiatt/Getty Images for Aeropostale; 39 Bethany chat icon: Timothy Hiatt/Getty Images for Aeropostale; 39 Obama chat icon: EdStock/iStockphoto; 41: Adam Taylor/ABC via Getty Images; 42: Astrid Stawiarz/Getty Images for Go Red; 43: Kevin Mazur/Getty Images.

Library of Congress Cataloging-in-Publication Data

Names: Morreale, Marie.
Title: Bethany Mota / by Marie Morreale.
Description: New York : Children's Press, 2016. | Series: Real bios | Includes bibliographical references and index.
Identifiers: LCCN 2015029463| ISBN 9780531223789 (library binding) | ISBN 9780531225622 (pbk.)
Subjects: LCSH: Mota, Bethany, 1995---Juvenile literature. | Internet personalities--Biography--Juvenile literature. | Fashion designers--United States--Biography--Juvenile literature.
Classification: LCC CT275.M6537 M67 2016 | DDC 746.9/2092 --dc23 LC record available at http://lccn.loc.gov/2015029463

Printed in the United States 113
SCHOLASTIC, CHILDREN'S PRESS, and associated logos are trademarks and/or registered trademarks of Scholastic Inc.

1 2 3 4 5 6 7 8 9 10 R 25 24 23 22 21 20 19 18 17 16

Bethany loves sharing her beauty and lifestyle tips with her fans.

# MEET BETHANY!

## THE YOUTUBE SUPERSTAR SHINES

Believe it or not, Internet sensation Bethany Mota has more YouTube subscribers than pop stars such as Lady Gaga or Selena Gomez. She also has more Instagram followers than fashion magazines *Vogue*, *Elle*, *Marie Claire*, *Glamour*, and *Cosmopolitan* combined!

Bethany has traveled all over the world meeting and greeting her avid fans, who are known as Motavators. She shares her fashion favorites and makeup tips with everyone who is interested, and she learns from her fans, too. Bethany is more than just a style guru. She likes to call herself a lifestyle **vlogger**.

Born in 1995, Bethany has already lived a pretty amazing life. She has millions of fans, designs her own clothing line, is working on a music career, met and interviewed President Barack Obama, competed on *Dancing With the Stars*, and much more. If you want to learn more about what makes Bethany so special, check out this *Real Bio*. You will definitely become a Motavator!

# CONTENTS

By the time Bethany was 14, she was offering style advice from her bedroom on YouTube.

# BETHANY MOTA

# & YOUTUBE

## FROM LONELY GIRL TO SOCIAL MEDIA ICON

I n 1995, Tony and Tammy Mota were living in the small town of Los Banos, California, when their second daughter, Bethany, was born. Tony was an electrical engineer, and Tammy was a stay-at-home mom. They were a happy family who enjoyed taking trips to visit family and explore new places.

Today, Bethany admits that she was a bit of a handful when she was a toddler. "I would pull my sister's hair down to the floor, and she cried and called for our mom," Bethany told Web site intanputrikirana .blogspot.com. Sibling antics aside, the Mota family was very close.

Bethany was homeschooled by Tammy until the third grade. After that, she attended public school. Bethany loved being in school with other students . . . until middle school, that

**Her Style**
Daring . . .
Girly . . .
Bam!

One of the most in-demand vloggers, Bethany visits Sirius XM radio studios for an in-person interview.

All smiles, Bethany attended the 2014 VidCon in Anaheim, California.

is. She has confessed that middle school was the "worst experience" of her life. For some reason, girls she thought were her friends turned into mean girls. Bethany, who had loved communicating with her BFFs online, discovered that a fake MySpace page had been created in her name. It was full of pictures of her and nasty comments. "The captions were written to sound like I was making fun of myself, like, 'Oh, my God, I'm so ugly,'" she told *Seventeen* magazine. "It got to me. I didn't want to hang out with my friends or go anywhere. I had so much **anxiety** and struggled to be in situations with people. I wasn't eating a lot, like, maybe one meal a day."

The cyberbullying also turned several of Bethany's good friends against her. Up until that point, Bethany had been an outgoing, positive person. She took dance, acting, and voice lessons. She also appeared in school plays and was totally adventurous. But once the bullying started, she retreated into herself. "All I wanted to do was sit in bed all day," she told intanputrikirana .blogspot.com. "I couldn't do anything. I was just really upset, really sad. I had really negative thoughts all the time and it really affected me."

To avoid the difficulties with her classmates, Bethany went back to being homeschooled. When she wasn't studying, she started exploring the Internet. "I didn't want to talk to anyone; I didn't want to leave my house," Bethany told *Business Insider*. "[YouTube] was kind of an outlet for me to be myself and not really worry about what anyone thought."

Bethany shares YouTube "secrets" with fellow vloggers, style guru Michelle Phan and baking queen Rosanna Pansino.

"I LIKE . . . EDGINESS WITH THE MORE **BOHEMIAN**, GIRLY THINGS."

Bethany soon became interested in the online beauty blog and vlog community. She loved watching the do-it-yourself (DIY) fashion and makeup videos posted by girls who were just like her. It was fun to watch YouTube videos where girls showed off the things they had bought on recent shopping trips and offered tips on finding bargains and putting together different looks. "It was so cool seeing girls being positive and spreading happiness," Bethany told *Seventeen*.

At age 13, Bethany decided to get in on the YouTube fun. "[It took] a lot because going from feeling so

Bethany showed off some of her hot picks at the 2014 Unleash YouTube event.

Bethany and fellow YouTube personality Tyler Oakley laugh it up and play dress-up at a YT event.

insecure and then literally putting myself out there for the world to see was a huge step," Bethany revealed on *The Ellen DeGeneres Show*. "The first video . . . it was like me talking about different makeup products, which is funny because I was never really much of a girly-girl, but I kind of just found it fun and I kind of got into the beauty and fashion world through YouTube."

Bethany's mom was very supportive. She brought home bags of makeup and accessories, took Bethany for mall hauls, and encouraged her daughter to experiment. Bethany started her first YouTube channel, Macbarbie07, in 2009. Her first video included M-A-C cosmetic products and goodies from makeup megastore

BETHANY'S SISTER, BRITTANY, ONCE TAUGHT HER TO SLURP KOOL-AID THROUGH HER NOSE WITH A STRAW. OW!

Because Bethany has so many followers, she is one of the most in-demand speakers on social media.

Sephora. It was definitely a DIY production! Bethany didn't have a **tripod**, so she put her camera on a stack of books and boxes. "At first, I made beauty videos that were like everyone else's—I'd try to act perfect," she told *Seventeen*. "But then I realized it might be more fun if I was just myself. So I showed my silly side and kept in the bloopers. I liked those videos way more, and people appreciated the realness."

After a while, Bethany started to feel more comfortable in front of the camera. She loved the fact that she was doing everything—shooting the videos, editing them, and uploading the final product. And what she loved most was the interaction she had with her ever-growing audience. "I just couldn't believe there were 100 people out there listening to me," Bethany explained to finance.yahoo.com. "It was a great feeling."

Bethany let her creative juices flow. Her videos included mall hauls, makeup and hair tutorials, what's-in-my-purse peeks, room tours, and even a Katy Perry Halloween costume tutorial. One hundred viewers became one million . . . and then even more! Bethany

Fans show off autographed photos of Bethany at a meet-and-greet with her.

was shocked at the response she got to a video tour of her bedroom—three months after it went online, it already had more than 6 million views!

"It's no secret I love sharing details about my bedroom," Bethany told *Tiger Beat* magazine. "The color palette is pink, white, and gold, with an emphasis on white (because all my furniture is white), but I have hints of pink and gold to bring in a slightly bohemian feel. I spend a lot of time in my room—editing videos, reading emails, or researching new ideas—so I purposely

# FACT FILE

## THE BASICS

MAMA-MOTA
"Bethany was my little tomboy!"

**FULL NAME:** Bethany Noel Mota

**NICKNAMES:** Beth, Bethers, Betherson, Macbarbie

**BIRTHDAY:** November 7, 1995

**ASTROLOGICAL SIGN:** Scorpio

**BIRTHPLACE:** Los Banos, California

**PARENTS:** Tammy and Tony Mota

**OLDER SISTER:** Brittany Mota Wiley

**NIECE:** Marin Wiley

**HERITAGE:** Mexican and Portuguese

**PET:** Dog named Winnie

**CELEBRITY CRUSH:** Dave Franco

**GUILTY PLEASURE:** Instagram

**FANS:** Motavators

**YOUTUBE CHANNELS:** Macbarbie07 and BethanysLife

decorated it to have a really comforting vibe."

In March 2010, Bethany started her second YouTube channel, BethanysLife. Its videos follow Bethany as she does everyday stuff and meets with her true-blue Motavators. Little did Bethany Noel Mota know that her YouTube personality and dedication to her fans would lead to much, much more. Though she started out as a lonely, anxious 13-year-old who didn't want to leave her bedroom, Bethany opened the doors and blossomed into a social media icon.

## FAVORITES

"I'M A PERFECTIONIST."

**FASHION INSPIRATIONS:**
Lauren Conrad, Vanessa Hudgens, Selena Gomez, and Kendall Jenner

**MOVIE QUOTE:**
"Crushed it!"— Rebel Wilson in Pitch Perfect

**COLOR:** Pink

**HOLIDAY:** Christmas

**FLOWER:** Sunflower

**FASHION STORES:** PacSun, Forever 21, Urban Outfitters

**ANIMAL:** Owl

**TV SHOWS:** Once Upon a Time and Pretty Little Liars

**DECORATIVE ITEM:** Accent pillows

**SOCIAL MEDIA:** YouTube, Instagram

**MOVIES:** Frozen and Despicable Me

Lauren Conrad

Selena Gomez

Bethany rocked as *ET* reporter at the 2014 Nickelodeon Kids' Choice Awards!

# BETHANY MOTA TAKES ON THE WORLD

## FROM MIDDLE CLASS GIRL TO MILLIONAIRE

"Hi, I'm Bethany. I'm a YouTuber!" This is how Bethany often introduces her vlogs. Of course, if you are tuning in to the Macbarbie07 or BethanysLife channels, you already know exactly who Bethany Mota is. She's the girl next door, your BFF who is visiting in your bedroom, and a social media superstar! When Bethany first started posting YouTube videos, it was a hobby. But before she knew it, her YouTube presence became a career—a very successful one!

> "MY VIEWERS ARE MY BESTIES AND I LOVE THEM BUNCHES!"

Bethany had no idea that her YouTube videos would turn into anything more than a good way to pass the time. However, in 2016, her YouTube subscribers nudged the 10 million mark, her Instagram account boasted around 6 million followers, and she had almost 3 million Twitter followers!

How did it happen? Well, at first her business plan was just to be herself. "I started out doing strictly makeup and then I went into fashion and hair," she told the *Wall Street Journal*. "I started sprinkling different topics in. I don't consider myself a beauty or fashion guru. It's more of a lifestyle that represents me, who I am, and my likes and interests. If I had to pick a favorite kind of video, I like just doing one that incorporates everything. So I'll pick a topic, like a summer-theme, and I'll do a video on hairstyle, makeup, outfit and a cooking video all in one."

How does Bethany pick and choose which products or styles to feature? It's not surprising that lots of makeup and fashion companies want Bethany to show off their merchandise. "A lot of brands will e-mail me and say, 'Hey can you try out my products?'" she told myfoxny.com. "I'll always say, 'I'm open to trying products,' but I'm just very

## Bethany's Timeline

### Bethany's Dreams Come True

**JUNE 8, 2009**
Bethany creates her first YouTube channel, Macbarbie07

**MARCH 21, 2010**
Bethany launches her second YouTube Channel, BethanysLife

**JULY 30, 2012**
Bethany posts her first ROOM TOUR!!! video

At *Variety*'s Massive: The Entertainment Marketing Summit, Bethany shared her social media knowledge.

picky about it because you know at the end of the day I really want my viewers to think they can trust me."

Bethany's reputation is important to her. She wants to make sure that her viewers know that she stands behind the products she shares on her vlogs. "I will never talk about something or promote something that I don't actually use and that I don't care about because with the relationship being so strong between the creators and viewers, they can see when you don't truly like something," she explained when she appeared as a

**DECEMBER 8, 2013**
Bethany launches her clothing line for Aéropostale

**MARCH 29, 2014**
Bethany serves as *Entertainment Tonight*'s reporter at the 2014 Nickelodeon's Kids' Choice Awards

guest speaker at *Variety*'s Massive: The Entertainment Marketing Summit. "As long as you're honest and truthful, then that's what builds that relationship. And the stronger that is, the more they're going to listen to what you say."

Bethany's social media success created a whole career for her. Because she was reaching such a large audience of young people, many companies wanted to have her as part of their businesses. Bethany had to stop a moment and think. Her first move was to make her dad, Tony, her manager. He helps her go through all the offers she gets. However, it is Bethany who makes the final decisions about who she teams up with. In 2013, the fashion line Aéropostale approached her to develop a brand line for them. In December 2013, she did just that. The line includes clothes such as dresses, graphic tees, hoodies, and sweaters; accessories such as bags, scarves, and fragrances; and

**JULY 28, 2014**
Bethany launches her first perfume, xoxo Beth

**AUGUST 10, 2014**
Bethany wins a Teen Choice Award for Web Star: Fashion and Beauty

Motavators cheered as Bethany made an appearance for her clothing line at an Aéropostale store.

lifestyle products such as sheets, pillows, rugs, and lamps!

Bethany has also stretched into the music business. She released her first single, "Need You Right Now" in October 2014. It reached number four on the iTunes charts. Even Kevin Jonas tweeted that he was a fan and congratulated her!

"I really want to dive into music now," Bethany told

**AUGUST 14, 2014**
Bethany is a guest judge on *Project Runway*

**SEPTEMBER 7, 2014**
Bethany wins a Streamy Award for her fashion program

**SEPTEMBER 15, 2014**
Bethany joins season 19 of *Dancing With the Stars*

**OCTOBER 2014**
Bethany graces the cover of the October 2014 *Seventeen* magazine

On *Dancing With the Stars'* Movie Night, Bethany and partner Derek Hough danced to the title song from *Singin' in the Rain.*

the Web site JustJaredJr.com when the single first came out. "I've been wanting to get into music for three or four years now—to do covers or write songs. And now with the single out there, I feel like that was the perfect way to introduce my musical side to my audience and everyone else. I'm very relieved because I've been anticipating it so much. Now that it's on iTunes, I feel

**OCTOBER 13, 2014**
Bethany releases her first single, "Need You Right Now"

**OCTOBER 13, 2014**
Bethany is ranked sixth on *Time* magazine's 25 Most Influential Teens of 2014 list

**JANUARY 22, 2015**
Bethany interviews President Barack Obama

like I can work on writing my own songs. Obviously, that's going to take time, but it's definitely something I'm working on."

Perhaps it was Bethany's love of music that encouraged her to participate in ABC's *Dancing With the Stars* in September 2014. The competition was Bethany's TV debut, and she had a fantastic time. She and her partner, Derek Hough, reached the finals and made it all the way to fourth place. "Oh my gosh! It's blowing my mind," Bethany told Ryan Seacrest when she visited his radio show, *On Air With Ryan Seacrest*. "I didn't even think I was going to make it past Week 1. I thought I was going home."

Well, Bethany didn't go home. In fact, since becoming a big star, she hardly sees her home at all. She's always traveling. China . . . Japan . . . Europe . . . New York . . .

**Number One**

Bethany was the most Googled fashion designer in 2014!

**MARCH 5, 2015**
Bethany is included in *Time* magazine's 30 Most Influential People on the Internet

**JULY 27, 2015**
Bethany launches her second perfume, Love Bethany

Washington, D.C.—no place is too far or too near. "It's a lot of traveling, but that's the best part!" she told *Tiger Beat* magazine. "I'm lucky that through doing what I love, I've been able to travel the world, meet my audience and work with amazing people. I even got to meet the President of the United States!"

That's right! Bethany and fellow YouTubers GloZell Green and Hank Green got to go to the White House to interview President Obama.

Though she is still young, Bethany has already had many fantastic opportunities. She credits YouTube and her Motavators with it all. It's been quite a ride. "I do talk about beauty and fashion . . . some

**"I'VE ALWAYS MADE IT A POINT TO BE KIND TO PEOPLE."**

people might see it as kind of **superficial**, but in the end my main goal for what I do is to kind of just promote self-love and self-confidence and taking a bad situation and making it into something amazing," Bethany explained on *The Ellen DeGeneres Show*. "Because you can see the process. I've been doing videos for six years. I haven't deleted any. You can see me when I was making my first video. I was really shy and really closed off and I grew and I really learned so much about myself, and I've really learned the importance of not worrying about other people's opinions."

Bethany's growth is something she is determined to share with her viewers. What's her main lesson? Be confident and be yourself. Bethany feels that YouTube was the means for her to get to that point in her life. "I think it's made me be a lot more self-motivated and has taught me how to encourage myself and not rely on a teacher or a boss telling me what to do," she told *Seventeen*. "I'm my own boss. My biggest thing to overcome has been not being afraid to be different. It's safer to do what everyone else is doing, but it pays off way more to be yourself."

In 2014, Bethany was interviewed by host Savannah Guthrie on *Today*.

Bethany gets a
touch-up before
the Go Red For
Women event.

# BETHANY TALKS . . . MOTAVATORS LISTEN!

## THE YOUTUBE SUPERSTAR SHARES HER TIPS, EXPERIENCES, AND DREAMS WITH YOU

Find out what Bethany says about the importance of YouTube, her love of music, why she wants to share her girl-power message with her viewers, and much, much more! Read on . . . bet she answers some of your questions!

### On being friends with other YouTubers . . .

"Yes . . . [like] Ricky Dillon. I met him through YouTube. . . . It's cool because we can talk about YouTube and he gets it. Most of the time, those YouTube friendships start online—like through DMing on Twitter. Then we will get each other's numbers and start texting and hanging out in person."

Behind the scenes with Bethany at a social media event

## On preparing for her busy schedule . . .

"Getting things done the night before a crazy day! This has helped me so much when I have to be up early and don't want to be late. Simple things like packing your bag, organizing your makeup station, and planning your outfit at night can shave off tons of time in the morning."

## On girl power . . . "My best advice to girls who want to be powerful is don't be afraid to be different. When I was younger I always tried to fit in with everyone else, and when I realized that I can just be myself I felt so much better and I felt so much more confident."

## On having powerful girls as role models . . .

"I think it's important to have powerful girls as role models. When I was young, I went through bullying and all I really needed at that point was someone to tell me everything was going to be OK and someone to help me out. And that's what I want to be for other girls."

## On her own role model . . .

"The first person [who] pops in my head is my mom. Ever since I was younger, I've always looked up to her. She's so strong and she still inspires me every day."

WOW! Confidence is the basis of being positive.

Bethany loves to answer her fans' questions.

**The first thing she would buy with a million dollars . . .** "Oh my gosh. This is so hard. I'd probably buy like a huge island, and then, like, all of my viewers could be on that island and it'd be made out of candy. Why not?"

**On a cool DIY project for beginners:** "One of my go-to items for DIY is a Mason jar. They are so versatile and the opportunities to create something with them are endless. You can grab some acrylic paint that matches your room and paint the entire jar for a new flower vase, or fill it with glass beads and use it to hold your makeup brushes."

Bethany always gives 100 percent of herself to her projects.

**What she would like to change about herself . . .** "I stress myself out because everything that I have to do has to be perfect in my eyes or else I go insane."

## What she learned from her *Dancing With the Stars* partner, Derek Hough . . .

"Probably to try new things. That's why I wanted to do that competition. Because it scared me so much—performing live and everything—having him as a teacher, he really pushes me to do all of these things that don't really come naturally to me. Comparing now to my first rehearsal, I wasn't as in control of my body as I am now. I wasn't aware of things like my posture and having a strong core. And now they are things I do naturally thanks to him. He trained me to present myself that way."

According to Bethany, Derek taught her more than dance moves.

## On the music she listens to . . .

"I listen to a lot of different people actually. I have a Spotify account, so it's really easy for me to find smaller artists and people who may not be at the top of the charts, but have really cool music. I love Banks. She's one of my favorite artists by far. Tove Lo is one I've been listening to recently. I've listened to Lorde for the past couple of years now. She's awesome. That's the vibe that I listen to . . . somewhat dark, a lot of indie stuff, acoustic, and very raw—is my favorite kind of music."

## On interviewing President Barack Obama . . .

"It was scary. . . . We actually did a rehearsal the day before because we wanted to make sure we had all our questions ready and we knew what we were going to say. So they had a fake president so we [could] go over the questions with the fake president. . . . The fake president comes up to me and I start shaking uncontrollably, like getting so nervous. And then I pause and I'm like, 'Bethany, this is not even the real president. Like you need to calm down. What are you going to do tomorrow for the real interview?' But the actual experience, it went so well. It was so fun. And I got a selfie with the president."

**POTUS**
During her chat with the president, Bethany learned these initials mean "President Of The United States."

## How she likes to relax . . .

"I like to darken the lights and go on Tumblr or Pinterest and just scroll. I also like to write out my thoughts—that's something I've been doing a lot of. If there's anything I'm going through, writing it down makes it better. I can vent without having to worry that someone will tell other people."

## On her close friends . . .

"In my whole life I've had three or four best friends. A friendship is like a commitment and you can't just be like, 'Oh, yeah! I'm your friend!' You have to be there for them. I like having a small number of close friends, so I can focus on them."

**How her fans influence her . . .** "My collection has always been very much inspired by my viewers. So many of them have told me that my style gives them ideas, but they do just the same for me. I love being engaged with my audience because they are all so unique and creative. Whenever I need some help designing, I love just sending a tweet out asking my viewers what they want. My collection is for them, so I want to make sure they love what I'm putting out."

Motavators come in all ages, and Bethany loves every one of them!

# BETHANY'S
# LOOK BOOK

## FAB FACTS, FUN STUFF, QUICK QUOTES, LOTSA LISTS & MORE!

## YUMMY YUMMY

**FOODIE WISH**
UNLIMITED PIZZA

**COMFORT FOOD**
MAC AND CHEESE,
SANDWICHES

**FAVORITE DRINKS**
STARBUCKS PASSION TEA
LEMONADE, GREEN TEA

**QUICK SNACK**
FRENCH FRIES

**MINTS**
GREEN TEA–
FLAVORED MINTS

**DREAM DIY
PROJECT**
TO DESIGN HER OWN
KITCHEN

**FAST FOOD**
BURGER KING,
MCDONALD'S,
MENCHIE'S, STARBUCKS,
TACO BELL, YOGURTLAND

**FAVORITE FRUIT**
RASPBERRIES

# FASHION PASSION

**GO-TO OUTFIT:** Skater skirt, crop top, and combat boots

**VANESSA HUDGENS:** "She really masters that bohemian vibe."

**COMFORT STYLE:** Overalls

**FAVORITE DIY CLOTHES:** "Graphic tees with witty sayings and cool graphics"

**PERSONAL STYLE:** Comfortable, bohemian, laid-back

**FAVORITE STORES FOR SUPER FINDS:** Thrift shops, flea markets, and antique stores

**SOCKS:** "Knee-high socks are awesome because they keep your legs warm and allow you to wear dresses and skirts in the cold weather."

**FASHION HAULS:** Crop tops and high-waisted skirts and pants

**HATS:** Fedoras—great for a bad hair day

**MUST-HAVE MAKEUP:** Mascara

"I LIKE TAKING AN IDEA OF SOMETHING THAT IS TRENDY AND MAKING IT MY OWN."

# BETHANY & PRESIDENT OBAMA CHAT

In January 2015, President Barack Obama sat down with three young YouTube journalists, comedian GloZell Green, Internet "nerd" Hank Green, and fashion guru Bethany Mota. Here's a snippet of Bethany's Q&A with the president.

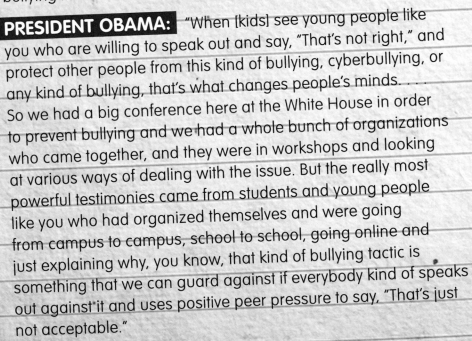

**BETHANY:** "When I was younger I was cyberbullied, which affected me in a very big way. . . . How can we just prevent that, prevent bullying in schools and online?"

**PRESIDENT OBAMA:** "When [kids] see young people like you who are willing to speak out and say, "That's not right," and protect other people from this kind of bullying, cyberbullying, or any kind of bullying, that's what changes people's minds. . . . So we had a big conference here at the White House in order to prevent bullying and we had a whole bunch of organizations who came together, and they were in workshops and looking at various ways of dealing with the issue. But the really most powerful testimonies came from students and young people like you who had organized themselves and were going from campus to campus, school to school, going online and just explaining why, you know, that kind of bullying tactic is something that we can guard against if everybody kind of speaks out against it and uses positive peer pressure to say, "That's just not acceptable.""

**BETHANY:** "So my audience had a lot of fun questions for you, so we're going to do a quick lightning round. [First] if you have any free time, what TV show or movies do you watch?"

**PRESIDENT OBAMA:** "You know, I'm really big on sports. So, the truth of the matter is that I'm mostly watching SportsCenter . . . Whenever I'm working out in the gym, if there's a basketball game or football game on, I'm usually tuned in there."

**BETHANY:** "What did you want to be, growing up?"

**PRESIDENT OBAMA:** "I wanted to be a bunch of different things. I wanted to be an architect for a long time. . . . And I suppose in the back of my mind at some point I thought that playing in the NBA would be great, being a basketball player. That ended I think around the age of 13 when I realized I wasn't talented enough."

**BETHANY:** "And the last one is, if you had any superpower, what would it be?"

**PRESIDENT OBAMA:** "Any superpower . . . you know, I guess like the flying thing seems pretty cool, right? Sort of zipping around . . . as long as you could stay warm. The invisibility thing seems a little sneaky to me. You know, it's like, what are you going to be doing with that? You're going to be listening in on people's conversations. So I guess the flying thing. One time somebody asked me this and I gave an answer that my wife, Michelle, teased me . . . she thought this was really nerdy. But it's OK. I'll go ahead and tell you anyway. I don't know if this is a superpower. I'd love to be able to speak any language . . . I would love . . . like anybody I met anywhere in the world I could just talk in their language. To me that would be really cool."

**BETHANY:** "I would love that too."

**PRESIDENT OBAMA:** "Isn't that a cool one?"

# DANCING WITH DEREK

When Bethany competed on *Dancing With the Stars*, she was partnered with four-time winner Derek Hough. They were nicknamed Team Berek! It was a match made in dance floor heaven! Though they didn't win season 19, they did make a BFF match!

## BETHANY ON DEREK:

"Derek is incredible. I mean honestly, I got the best partner. He's absolutely an amazing choreographer and everything. I think it's that, I didn't believe in myself. I was like, 'There is no way I can do this,' because yes, he's an awesome teacher, but the student also has to put in the work."

"This guy is by far one of the most inspiring people I have ever met. Derek, you have been such a positive part of my life these past few months. Your passion for life and creativity in everything you do never cease to amaze me. Watching the way you visualize incredible ideas and bring them to life is beyond fascinating and I am honored to have been able to be a part of it for a while. Thank you for everything. You are one very beautiful person. Love you @derekhough."

"I'VE DISCOVERED THINGS ABOUT MYSELF THAT, THINGS I NEVER THOUGHT I COULD DO!"—BETHANY

## DEREK ON BETHANY:

"Bethany, definitely for me, has had the most dramatic journey and evolution throughout the season, which has been amazing to watch and see her grow."

"She got over a lot of adversity that we didn't even show on TV, on camera. Injuries that we didn't play to the camera. . . . She really hid it and we kept it to ourselves and she was strong. She was a warrior. She was amazing and I was just really, really proud of her for that."

Bethany and Derek were definitely *DWTS* fan faves!

Bethany gave Derek a high-tech camera to thank him for his *DWTS* support!

"I went to Sydney Australia, and I saw the impact of what she makes on all these young girls, they call themselves the Motavators. It's been amazing to go into her world and see, you know, her influence."

Bethany sends her love!

# TODAY'S ROLE MODEL . . . TOMORROW'S MEDIA MOGUL?
## BETHANY REACHES FOR THE STARS!

"I think it's really cool that girls look up to me, not just for fashion, but when I do meet-ups, there have been girls that come up to me in tears and [are] emotional saying that I inspired them with personal issues and self-confidence and that just warms my heart," Bethany told a reporter at the 2014 Playlist Live event. "It just shows that on my YouTube channel I'm just being myself. . . . I'm just being who I am and they seem to appreciate that and, also, they inspire me as well. It's kind of this really cool friendship and I feel like we can just be ourselves and be who we are—as cheesy as that sounds."

It's hardly cheesy, Bethany! Motavators really do appreciate Bethany's down-to-earth approach to the tips and messages she is spreading. It is also obvious that she didn't get into YouTube to become a social media superstar. At first it was just for fun, but when it looked as if it was going to really take off, Bethany put her serious cap on and got down to the hard work of building a business. "A lot of people have asked me, 'How do you become a successful YouTuber?'," she told Cosmopolitan.com. "That's the wrong question to ask because it's so much hard work, and if you don't genuinely love the process of creating and working hard, then I think it's very easy to get burned out on it. It definitely takes a lot of dedication and a lot of time."

*Dedication* is the key word for Bethany. She believes in every project she takes on. She won't put her name on anything that doesn't meet

**Life Advice**
"Take those risks!"

Bethany encourages you to go after what you love to do.

the quality standards she has set for herself. And she isn't afraid to try something new. "I'm always looking for ways that I can improve what I do based on what I have done in the past," she revealed to fashionista.com. "I think this is a good mindset to have because it allows my content to get better with time. I don't really focus on trying to stand out. I think that as long as you be yourself, that will happen naturally."

As Bethany's influence has grown, she has realized that she has a responsibility to her fans. She is serious about everything she shares with her viewers, and that includes her positive attitude. This all got started because Bethany was cyberbullied, and that experience is never far from her mind. In 2015, Bethany partnered with PACER's, the national bullying prevention organization. Since 2006, PACER's has provided concrete, real-life programs to encourage and inspire kids to fight bullying in their schools and communities. It is a perfect connection for Bethany. She explained to Ellen DeGeneres, "We're still in the beginning stages, but just any way that I can really inspire my viewers to love themselves is my main goal."

**"ONLINE, I'M MY OWN DIRECTOR, MY OWN PRODUCER."**

As for Bethany's life goals, she's not afraid of taking risks. She wants to explore her musical side a bit more. She recently told *J-14* magazine, "I'm working on music . . . possibly an album. As of right now I only have a couple of songs in the works. I released my single last year, but it was very pop sounding, and now I'm kind of changing my musical style a little bit. Making it more stripped down and a little bit more acoustic sounding. . . . It's kind of like a new world. I'm very unfamiliar with it, and that's what gets me excited. Diving into things that are so unfamiliar and being able to create something. . . . The idea of a song not existing and then you writing it and making it a thing is amazing. So I'm just hoping that my audience really loves it."

"I DON'T WANT TO DO SOMETHING UNLESS IT FEELS ORGANIC. TRUE TO ME, WHO I AM AND WHAT MY CHANNEL REPRESENTS."

What are her plans for 5 or 10 years from now? As usual, Bethany is practical but positive. She told Yahoo! Makers, "Six years ago I would've never even guessed that I would be in this position now. No matter what, I just want to continue connecting with my viewers and being creative. I'm able to create through YouTube, music, clothing and more. I would love to continue doing all of those things."

And if that means taking more risks, so be it. "Sometimes the things that we are afraid of are the things that can change our lives and make us stronger," Bethany says.

# Resources

## BOOKS

Klein, Emily. *From Me to YouTube: The Unofficial Guide to Bethany Mota.* New York: Scholastic 2015.

McGuire, Jo. *128 Facts About Bethany Mota: For True Motavators Only.* Seattle: Amazon Digital Services 2015.

## ARTICLES

"Bethany Mota! How She Silences Bullies & Found Her Voice on YouTube," *Seventeen* October 2014.

"YouTube Star Bethany Mota Redefines Style For Millennials," *Latina* August 2015.

# Facts for Now

Visit this Scholastic Web site for more information on **Bethany Mota**: www.factsfornow.scholastic.com
Enter the keywords **Bethany Mota**

# Glossary

**anxiety** *(ang-ZYE-uh-tee)* strong feelings of worry or fear

**bohemian** *(boh-HEE-mee-uhn)* unconventional and artistic

**superficial** *(soo-pur-FISH-uhl)* concerned only with what is obvious or on the surface; not deep or thorough

**tripod** *(TRY-pahd)* a stand with three legs that is used to steady a camera or other piece of equipment

**vlogger** *(VLAH-gur)* someone who creates video blogs, or vlogs

# Index

# Acknowledgments

**Page 6:** As a toddler: intanputrirana.blogspot.com February 10, 2014

**Page 8:** Fake MySpace page: *Seventeen* September 2014

**Page 9:** Stay in bed all day: intanputrirana.blogspot.com

**Page 9:** YouTube interest: *Business Insider* January 18, 2014

**Page 9:** Edginess: JustJaredJr.com October 27, 2014

**Page 10:** Positive videos on YT: *Seventeen* September 2014

**Page 10:** Start on YT: *The Ellen DeGeneres Show* April 7, 2015

**Page 12:** Real-life videos: *Seventeen* September 2014

**Page 13:** 100 viewers: finance.yahoo.com April 21, 2014

**Page 14:** Bethany's bedroom: *Tiger Beat* May 2015

**Page 14:** Mama-Mota: YouTube—videosrex.com

**Page 16:** Perfectionist: Aéropostale Interview November 19, 2013

**Page 19:** "Hi, I'm Bethany!": *Daily Mail* January 19, 2014

**Page 19:** Besties: *Daily Mail* January 19, 2014

**Page 20:** Favorite video: *Wall Street Journal* May 28, 2015

**Page 20:** Brands she uses: myfoxla.com February 14, 2014

**Page 21:** Brands she promotes: *Variety's* Massive: The Entertainment Marketing Summit, April 14, 2015

**Page 23:** First single: JustJaredJr.com October 27, 2014

**Page 25:** *Dancing With the Stars*: *On Air With Ryan Seacrest* November 21, 2014

**Page 26:** Traveling: *Tiger Beat* May 2015

**Page 26:** Being kind: *Latina* magazine August, 20, 2015

**Page 27:** Self-motivated: *Seventeen* September 2014

**Page 29:** On YT friends: *Seventeen* September 2014

**Page 30:** On being prepared: Yahoo.com July 20, 2015

**Page 30:** On girl power: RyanSeacrest.com September 10, 2014

**Page 31:** On role models: RyanSeacrest.com September 10, 2014

**Page 31:** On her role model: RyanSeacrest.com September 10, 2014

**Page 32:** On million-dollar purchase: Aéropostale Interview November 19, 2013

**Page 32:** On DIY beginner project: Yahoo.com July 20, 2015

**Page 32:** On change: Aéropostale Interview November 19, 2013

**Page 33:** On Derek Hough: JustJaredJr.com October 27, 2014

**Page 33:** On music: JustJaredJr.com October 27, 2014

**Page 34:** On interviewing President Obama: *The Ellen DeGeneres Show* April 7, 2015

**Page 34:** On how she relaxes: *Seventeen* September 2014

**Page 34:** On her close friends: *Seventeen* September 2014

**Page 35:** On fans influencing her: Yahoo.com July 20, 2015

**Page 37:** Fashion Passion—Vanesss Hudgens: Aéropostale Interview November 19, 2013

**Page 37:** Fashion Passion—Socks: teenfashion.about.com 2014

**Page 37:** Making it her own: Yahoo.com July 20, 2015

**Page 38:** President Obama interview: YouTube, Jan 22, 2015

**Page 40:** Derek is incredible: *On Air With Ryan Seacrest* November 21, 2014

**Page 40:** Inspiring guy: Enstars.com July 26, 2015

**Page 40:** Discovered things about myself: ABC News/*Good Morning America* November 24, 2014

**Page 41:** Bethany's evolution: *On Air With Ryan Seacrest* November 21, 2014

**Page 41:** Adversity: Celebrity.yahoo.com November 25, 2015

**Page 41:** Sydney reaction: Inquisitr.com November 25, 2014

**Page 42:** Being a role model: Playlist Live 2014

**Page 43:** Being a successful YouTuber: Cosmopolitan.com

**Page 43:** Life Advice: HollywoodTake.com November 25, 2014

**Page 44:** Looking to improve: fashionista.com January 20, 2014

**Page 44:** PACER's: *The Ellen DeGeneres Show* April 7, 2015

**Page 44:** Online: Inquisitr.com December 2014

**Page 45:** Music: J-14.com May 4, 2015

**Page 45:** Hard to predict: Yahoo! Makers July 20, 2015

**Page 45:** Feels organic: DailyMail.co.uk January 20, 2014

# About the Author

Marie Morreale is the author of many official and unofficial celebrity biographies. She attended New York University as an English/creative writing major and began her writing and editorial career in New York City. As the editor of teen/music magazines *Teen Machine* and *Jam!*, she covered TV, film, and music personalities and interviewed superstars such as Michael Jackson, Britney Spears, and Justin Timberlake/*NSYNC. Morreale was also an editor/writer at Little Golden Books.

Today, she is the executive editor, media, of Scholastic Classroom Magazines and writes about pop culture, sports, news, and special events. Morreale lives in New York City and is entertained daily by her two Maine coon cats, Cher and Sullivan.